DON'T FORGET TO BREATHE

DON'T FORGET TO BREATHE

CHRISTOPHER JAMES

LAGRANGE GEORGIA

iSeebookz Publishing
Suite 137B Commerce Ave #300
Lagrange GA 30241

 ISBN 979-8-9854863-7-7

First Edition
10 9 8 7 6 5 4 3 2 1

Printed in the United States

The information presented within this book is provided as an inspiration and for EDUCATIONAL PURPOSES ONLY. It is imperative that you seek consultation with a qualified healthcare professional for your specific individual requirements.

 To preserve the authenticity of the author's voice and the essence of inspired thoughts, minimal editing has been performed. We extend our gratitude for your support.

Christopher James/iSeebookz Publishing

Dedicated to

My loving mother, my son Christian,
and to all who made this book possible.

Contents

Copyright   iv

Dedication   v

1 The Holy Breath   1

2 Meditation   27

3 Ultimate Gratitude   47

4 Vibrations   67

5 Prayer   73

6 Power of Belief   79

7 The 30-Day Challenge   83

About The Author   89

References   91

1

The Holy Breath

Life for me began on a spring morning in Columbus, Ohio. A woman named Nina birthed Christopher into the world. It was then that I took my first breath of fresh air. Having spent 9 months in my mother's womb, living off the nutrients and oxygen she provided, now I could finally do it on my own.

We are all self-taught, and believe it or not, no one has to teach us how to breathe. But at some point, we learn that there are benefits to learning how to consciously breathe.

So, what is breathing consciously?

Now, before we get deep into the type of breathing I'm referring to, I would like to state that I am not a health specialist, nor am I a physician. I am simply a boy born in Ohio who, many years later, initially meditated for 30 days and discovered the holy breath.

Before meeting those 30 days of meditation, I had to experience enough life to appreciate the gift.

My childhood was interesting, to say the least. My Mother was married and had two children, myself and an older sister named Katrina, by one year. My sister lived with my Grandparents in my mother's hometown, Valdosta. I lived with my mother and stepdad in various places due to his active duty in the army. We (my mother & stepdad) didn't go too far and only bounced from Aurora, Colorado, to El Paso, Texas. Most of our time was spent in El Paso as we moved there twice, and that is also where my first school was located.

We traveled a lot outside of our daily lives. My stepdad's parents had a summer home on Fire Island that we would visit every year. We would also go to New York frequently since my step-grandmother lived in Manhattan. In this portion of my life, worries did not exist, and life as I knew it was perfect. All that would change upon me turning 12 years old when things took a turn with my mother and stepdad.

Once my mom and stepdad finally decided to call it quits, we drove 22 hours from El Paso, Texas, to Valdosta, Georgia, my mother's hometown. I believe it was then that reality first set in. The life that I lived prior to moving to Valdosta was very different. The man my mother was married to had parents who were very well off. Being their step-grandchild, they treated me like royalty and gave me an experience that all children should encounter. Truly.

Once we got to Valdosta, all of the glitz and glamour was gone. My mother was now a single parent, and it was all on her. Now, she did a wonderful job, but the summerhouse on Fire Island and trips to Manhattan to see Grandma were no more. My mother always worked extremely hard and provided for my sister and me. And I appreciate my mother for the knowledge that was given to me throughout my life.

As I got into my teens, I started to be influenced by bad choices as I searched to find my purpose. Fascinated by Scarface and Mafia movies, I gravitated to that type of activity in the real world. The environment that I was in also bred that type of behavior. Growing up as young boys, we were all primitive in what we thought was a lawless world. My first hint of trouble would come during my 15th year for marijuana possession, but it was only a slap on the wrist. I was sent to a juvenile detention center in a town called Thomasville, Georgia.

The juvenile detention center was not a place for rehabilitation. The center was filled with kids my age, older and younger. All were lost in the attempts to figure out our life's purpose. The center had video games and basketball courts. We did have to go to class for a short period of time, but after that, it was pretty much play time until egos flared, and then violence would occur. After a few weeks at the Detention Center, I was released. Because of my legal representation, age, and lack of severity, the case was dropped and would not be on my record.

I was able to start working my first job at age 15. Prior to age 15, I made money by mowing yards around the neighborhood. My mother told me I should keep doing lawns since it was tax-free, but in my mind, I thought working a job would be better at the time.

Seek, and you shall find.

I started working as a cashier/ cook at a fast-food restaurant specializing in bite-size burgers. I worked my way up quickly and was promoted to master cashier and was making pretty decent for a kid in high school.

I want to walk you through my life and share these personal stories. So, you may understand my experience, where I come from, how changing my breathing and thoughts changed everything, for who I am today.

***

After 3 years of working and finishing high school, more substantial trouble would come.-"Irony is getting out of trouble, finding a job to stay out of trouble, then years later getting back into trouble only to get arrested at that same job."

So, shortly after graduation, upon turning 18, I found myself facing 12 years in prison due to an alleged kidnapping. The local police surrounded the fast-food restaurant I worked at while operating the drive-thru. Luckily, there was no one there as it was only the manager and me. They entered and quickly called out my name. When I came around the counter, and they put me in handcuffs, they tossed my apron across the counter as one of the detectives said, "You won't need this where you're going." As they took me outside, the parking lot was filled with police cars blocking the entrance and exit. I was put into the back of a police van and took me to the county jail for processing. At this time, I still did not know what I was being charged with.

After a few days in jail, I finally went to arraignment. I found out that I had been charged with kidnapping(felony), aggravated assault(felony), and possession of a firearm during the commission of a crime(felony). I was granted no bond.

So, I got a lawyer and sat. Jail was very different than the detention center. There were no video games or basketball courts, only concrete and bars.

Along with tiny windows that you could barely look out of to see the sunlight. The cells were small, with 3 to 4 men sleeping in bunk beds or boats. Boats are holders for beds that sit on the floor to allow more people to sleep in the rooms. Usually, rooms would hold 2 people, 1 in each bunk bed, but the boats allowed more, which sat on the floor. It was 23 hours of being locked in with men of all ages, attitudes of all sizes, people you had never met, people you have a history with, the good and bad, and the possibility of an hour out on the yard once a day, depending on how the correctional officers felt.

We were all piled up on top of each other in jail. I spent most of my time playing cards, chess & writing to pass the time. There was a lot of blank time in space, a period when I did not know what was going to happen with my life, but my faith has always made me fearless. Faith that I was not a bad person, only making bad choices, and no matter how it looked, I would make it through because of God's grace.

After serving 10 months at the county jail, I was found not guilty on the kidnapping charge and pleaded out to the lesser charges (Aggravated assault & possession of a firearm) using my first offender and PSI (pre-sentence investigation).

First offender is an act that allows first-time felony offenders to complete a period of time on probation to have the charge dismissed without it showing as a conviction.

As long as you do not get into any more trouble during the probation period, of course.

A pre-sentence investigation is when the court does a deep background check to decide your sentence.

It also means that one would have to submit a guilty plea in the blind, meaning you would not know your sentence until the investigation was complete. My lawyer recommended it to me because I never had an adult conviction. I did not have any previous criminal record prior to.

So, it was all in the hands of God. The courts counted the 10 months I was incarcerated as time served and sentenced me to an additional 7 months of incarceration at a probation detention center in a small town called Lakeland, Georgia. The Probation detention center was a prison.

Upon my entry, they shaved all the hair from my head and face and then placed me in a dorm with my peers. There was a wide range of types of people in this environment. People were from all over the state of Ga, and there weren't a lot of people from Valdosta. I didn't get into too many altercations while in the county jail, but here, it was different.

I was still young in years. I was arrested at 18 and experienced my 19th birthday incarcerated. Incarceration alters us in ways that we do not see. My mind and response to the world had changed drastically during this time. I felt as if I was only a boy before being arrested that day at work, and through the process, I was becoming a man.

The dorms were open, with about 60-70 people per dorm. There were 4 dorms at this camp. The people here were even more different than in jail. Here, everyone was already sentenced, and everyone was mixed in together, from people who had 10 years to people who had 10 months.

My assigned dorm was filled with young bucks like myself, full of energy that yearned for release. I got into many fights during this period due to the environment taking me back to an even more primitive nature. It wasn't until the last month that I finally started to slow down and get back to thoughts that were important.

Once I was released, I had served a total of 17 months incarcerated. I was to continue the time on probation. I was sentenced to 12 years of probation, 7 years for aggravated Assault, and 5 years for possession of a firearm, all running consecutively. (Back-to-back)

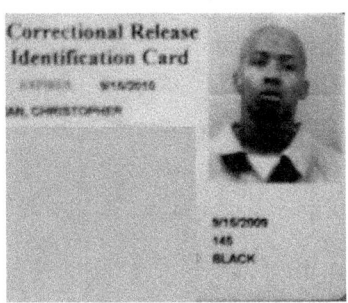

Early in my incarceration, my mother sent me the serenity prayer, and it was that prayer that got me through.

"God grant me the serenity
To accept the things, I cannot change;
Courage to change the things I can;
And wisdom to know the difference."

By now, I was back in reality with the opportunity to get ahead in life once again. My mother worked as a waitress at a local steakhouse restaurant and was able to get me an interview. I was open about my criminal history and was able to get hired on as a display cook.

About a year after my release, I was now 21, and I met back up with a childhood friend, and we started dating.

While dating, we had a beautiful boy of our own who took his first breaths on a fall morning, the same day as my mother's birthday. I was an adult now and needed to take care of not only myself but the new life I had created. I was back on the right track, but being incarcerated changed me. It made me an angry person. I was very combative.

Being in those types of environments, you learn quickly that you cannot take anything lightly, or it may display weakness. The last thing you want to do in there is look weak. Being institutionalized is a real thing, and I had to learn how to break the thought pattern. Jail takes people back to a more primitive nature, where everyone has to prove that they are tough, and anything said about you has to be addressed: true or false. For instance, if someone said they saw you take something from someone's room, and you did not- unless you address the person about the lie and fight the person over the lie, it will make you look weak to everyone else around.

Other people may take that as an invitation to extort. Remember, the last thing you want to do is look weak in jail and primitive because the things we would fight over to not look weak were worthless. Can you say…. Noodles and honeybuns? Nonetheless, that is a type of currency in those environments. It is also not about pretending to be tough because there are tougher guys who want to see how tough you are. The key in any situation is to just be yourself. Always take deep breaths and be comfortable in the skin God blessed you with at all times.

I hope any reader reading this does not have to ever experience incarceration because it is not a place that is necessary or good. If you have already or are currently…, I pray this book assists you on your journey to alter your thought pattern to a higher understanding of yourself so you may break the cycle and be free. Jail is not a place of rehabilitation. It makes us worse. People leave to come right back. The only ones who truly rehabilitate are the ones who can renew their minds regardless of the environment. Although it is not an easy task, and sometimes our environment will test us to see if we are better like we said we were. Especially when we feel as though we have failed those tests. If we still have breath in our lungs, then there is a lesson in every experience.

Breathe through it all.

The 3rd time is a charm…

I continued to work at the steakhouse for a while before obtaining a 2nd job at an upscale hotel as a cook. The hotel began to give me more hours and more pay than the steakhouse, so I eventually put in my 2 weeks' notice and thanked them for the opportunity. The hotel, not too long after, fired me for a disagreement between myself and a chef in the kitchen during rush hour. I feel, as if, it was unfair the way it was handled, but they fired me anyway.

What do you guys think?

One night, while working on backup, the chef (who was new) and another guy (who was new) were on the line. The line is where a person would cook all orders coming through. It was a hotel, but it also had a restaurant inside. Sometimes, it would get pretty busy. I would usually be the main cook on the line. I was one of the better cooks, but due to the fact that the new chef was friends with the new cook and (the new chef) making the schedule, that left me with fewer hours and on backup/prep. Backup is when you are mainly prepping food for the next day. You also have to thaw and take food to the line when called for.

The work day started slowly as I prepped in the back of the kitchen. Backup is given a list of food items to prep for the next day. At the front, the chef and new guy leaned on the counters, talking and laughing about who knows what. The restaurant started to get busy as I continued to prep. Shortly after, the cook from upfront calls out that he needs salmon.

Now, this is how this is supposed to work: when you take your last of something, you should either run and get a replacement immediately or call out to back up to bring one. However, you have to first make sure that your food drawer is stocked, and if it is low, let someone know.

We all come in at a decent time to check these things. The chef was with the new guy and knew how the protocol worked as well. I brought some salmon up, and the chef and the new cook were in the weeds. In the kitchen, "in the weeds" means someone is getting swamped with orders.

I immediately jumped in and noticed that the cook had not put any orders out and did not have any salmon previously except the salmon I had just brought out. Mind you, the salmon was also frozen and had to thaw. We worked out all the other orders, and 30-40 minutes later, we pushed out all the salmon orders.

In the end, the new guy thanked me for coming to his assistance. The chef, however, blamed me for the time it took to get the salmon out. I explained to him there was no salmon except for what I had brought out from the freezer, which he knew. He remembered it differently somehow because he called me into the office and attempted to write me up. I disagreed and refused to sign. I was not a disgruntled person with the chef. I respectfully told him that it made no sense and he should be looking at himself because he was on the line before it got busy and the line was not stocked.

I left that night without signing. About a week later, I was on a morning shift, and the chef was there once again. Upon finishing my shift, the chef, general manager & assistant manager called me into the office. It was in reference to the busy night. The chef told them his version of what happened and said that he feared for his life the night he told me he was writing me up. He said I got very confrontational with him, and it was my fault the line wasn't stocked; he said nothing about me pulling them out of the weeds.

The chef blatantly lied. I pleaded my case, but they had already made a decision. No one took into account that I was scheduled as backup, and the new guy and chef were the cooks on the line. Now I was angry. I took off my work shirt, leaving me only with a tank top on in the office. I tossed my work shirt and stormed out. I told them they were all crazy and accepted termination. If the chef were in jail with me back then, I would have had to fight the chef.

I was able to get unemployment after being fired, about 3 months passed, and corporate fired the chef & the general manager for financial misconduct. My breaking point came as I found trouble one last time. I was pulled over for speeding and found out I had a warrant for aggravated battery, which is a violent crime and a felony. Remember, I was still on probation for a violent crime, so this would indeed violate my first offender's probation if found guilty.

Here I was, once again being arrested and once again having my life threatened with years of more prison time. The court's offer was to revoke probation in full. Revoking Probation in full means that the time initially given on probation must be served through incarceration. So, the only option was to enter a guilty plea and accept the 12 years Incarcerated or take it to trial and prove my innocence. The year was 2012, and it felt like the beginning of something new. That time changed me tremendously in ways that I could not understand.

I arrived at the same jail I was placed in for months back when I was 18. This was almost 2 years after my release, and this time was very different. I knew in my heart that this was not my fate. There was no bond granted, and I again got a lawyer and sat. This time would be different. I did not have the same life with no responsibility. My son needed me. He needed me to be free to achieve purpose. I was not in relaxed mode, where I had 17 months to spend away from him. I needed to be free now. We had shared each other's side since his birth, and I did not want to change that now. My son gave me hope that I have a purpose to be great so that he may be greater. Help him in a way that no man helped me.

My father was not around in my life, and due to the split with my mother, I did not have a lot of direct male guidance in my life. My grandfather and uncles always modeled what men should be, but I always felt as if it was up to me to define who I am. I feel like the lack of a consistent father figure in my life attributed to my lack of respect for authority. I never had a father to fear, and my grandfather and I would have many heated debates when I was younger about things that we didn't agree on. Of course, to grandfather, there was no debate.

I have always been the type of person to stand firmly on what I believe, regardless of who sees it differently. However, respect was always displayed towards my grandfather because, as a youth, I still had a lot to learn. I learned how to be even more respectful and understanding with my grandfather. It was during this period of time that we developed a better relationship with love and understanding until the day he passed away.

My mind was different. I was not into the game of stooping down to the level of getting in the groove of doing time in jail. The correctional officers placed me in a prison dorm where the only way out was on a bus that takes you to diagnostics.

Diagnostics is where inmates are processed and shipped to different prisons.

During my first time incarcerated, I felt I couldn't let anything slide because it would make me look weak. This time, I didn't care about any of that. One day while in the Dayroom of the jail, I was on the phone with my mother. They had 3 phones in this dorm, and you got 15 mins per call. All 3 phones were filled (being used). Once I hung up the phone, this guy from upstairs started shouting to me, "Hey man, I was supposed to use that phone next." I looked at him crazy and told him to go use it. We began to argue back and forth, and he got to a point where he insinuated he wanted to fight. Now, the old me would have felt like I must prove I was not afraid.

But this new me that I was finding, said I don't have to prove anything, and I didn't want to join in that type of game. Not because I was afraid but because it was beneath me. I was very firm with him. I told him his best bet was to go lie down because if we fought, it wouldn't be pretty for him. We did not fight.

Not long after, the same guy would try to befriend me by offering me food and asking who my lawyer was. Even then, I refused to play the game. In my mind, I convinced myself that I would once again beat this crime I was being accused of. I told myself I would be out in 3 months. Now, this was considered crazy talk because, as I stated, the only way out of this dorm is through a bus to prison.

In the world we lived in, it never mattered if you did it or not. The only thing that ever matters is what you can prove. And if you don't fight for your rights, the system will process you guilty as charged every time.

I felt as if I was being tested to see if I could choose peace over chaos. I had a few situations where, in order to show my strength, I had to show restraint. After sitting for 2 months in jail, my lawyer got me a consultation with a guy named "Mr. Ohm," who had a new program. The name Ohm is important because it shows how God has everything lined up for us.

Understanding the ohm as a unit of electrical resistance in the international system of units can be empowering. The electrical frequency of one ampere (the flow of electricity) is proportional to the potential difference. In simpler terms, the greater the voltage, the greater the current of electricity.

"Om" is also the sound that monks will make during meditation. Our bodies have this same exact electrical resistance. We have a natural flow of electricity that flows within and surrounds us. Think of that static shock you may experience. That is your inner electricity. More than 99% of the body's electrical flow is at the skin. The resistance is measured in ohms.

Electricity is everywhere as all things are made of atoms with the smallest particle called electrons that create energy bonds. This particle called the atom-- makes up everything and every living being. As atoms connect to other atoms through electron bonding, they make up elements; elements make up living cells that organize to make you and continue to unify themselves to make the nervous system that conducts signals to allow you to do all that you do. Like, breathe. It is the connection of electricity flowing that sends messages throughout our body and expresses the life we live.

I did not realize until later that Mr. Ohm was God sending me a message to find peace. The program was usually intended for nonviolent offenders to be released on house arrest to serve time until their cases were decided. When I had this consultation with Mr. Ohm, he reviewed my history and denied my release. He looked me in the eyes and told me I was too violent and that the program was only for nonviolent offenders. That night, in my cell, I prayed like I had never prayed before. I have always had a relationship with God and have always prayed, but this prayer was different.

I prayed: "God, I know they are wrong. I know I am meant to be free and do not belong here. I know that I am to be free now, God." I believed it and felt it as if it were true. I repeated that all night as I paced back and forth in my cell.

The next morning, the guards called me out for visitation. I was under the impression my lawyer was there to tell me the next steps, but to my surprise, it was Mr. Ohm. He had papers to sign to finalize my release and told me I would be out within a week. They had accepted me for the house arrest program. He did not mention anything about the conversation the day before. I did not ask any questions, but I knew it was God. That day changed me and showed me more of the power of God that I have always known. With that release, I vowed to myself that I would never walk without God again.

The courts placed an ankle monitor around my ankle that could not be removed unless by the court. I had to charge it every night and shower with it. The rules of house arrest were extremely strict, as I could not even walk down the street or out the front yard. House arrest, however, gave me the opportunity to be present in the growth of my son. During my course of house arrest, I was able to work, so I started working at an Italian restaurant. Due to the blanks in my work history and criminal record at the time, they started me off as a dishwasher.

My days literally consisted of going to work and straight home with no exceptions, so I had a lot of time to think and gather my thoughts.

The trial date had finally arrived after 12 months of house arrest and was one of the most nerve-racking moments of my life. However, I learned to trust God in all moments, even when the future looked bleak. The serenity prayer stayed at the front of my brain. The odds did not look the greatest considering the circumstances, and everyone asked if I was sure that this was what I wanted to do. In my mind, it was the only thing I could do.

There were no deals, bargains, or pleas except guilty. If I had pled guilty, they would have revoked the 12 years of probation that I was serving, and I would serve the rest of my time in prison. After a few testimonies, including my own plea of innocence and mistaken identity, the jury deliberated for about an hour and returned with a not-guilty plea. I turned around to see my mother and sister smiling through their tears. The officers cut the ankle monitor off my leg in the courtroom, and I walked out with my head held high.

I was once again free…

Before I came to notice my breath, I started noticing patterns in my life and past patterns and numbers that aligned with them. For instance, I would count back my life 3 years and notice that some things back then I was encountering were very similar to what I was encountering at that moment. Then, I would lessen the years to see if there were any correlations between the two, and there were… At that time, I started to notice that I was going through similar situations each year during or close to that current season with different people.

I noticed 3 years prior to 2012, in 2009, that I was just being released from incarceration. Going back 2 years, dating the now mother of my child in 2010 was very similar to 2012, me being released and now us breaking up during the same months, just a different year. Same situations with different people or sometimes the same situation with the same people. The biggest same realization was myself. I was going through the same things because I was the one watching it all happen. I was stuck in a loop that I had to get out of. I was becoming truly aware of my actions. The direction I was going, and I realized someone had to grab the wheel.

Before I learned how to implement conscious breathing and other breathing techniques, my life was all over the place, and it felt as if I was not in control. However, through all of my hardships, I never once doubted that I would not make it out. I almost felt like it was not happening to me but that it was happening for me. I feel like it was all so that I could genuinely appreciate the gift I have now.

After the last hump of trouble, I decided I had spent enough time in Valdosta and would now relocate to Atlanta. While on house arrest, an ad popped up on TV about the Art Institute of Atlanta, and it piqued my interest. I have always been a lover and creator of music and felt that it was my destiny to pursue it. So, I decided I would move to Atlanta, enroll in school, and figure it out. I stayed in Valdosta for one more year to save money for my big move.

With my freedom, I picked up 2 more jobs on top of the restaurant to add income for the move. I was now cooking soup instead of washing dishes, working as a cook and a customer service rep at a marketing company. Working 3 jobs only leaves time to sleep in between work; everything seemed to be going well until my car broke down a few months before my move date.

The serenity prayer carried me through. I feel like that is one of the most important things to learn during this life. Things happen, and we cannot change them. The bigger question is, what do you do when it happens. My answer has always been simple, "Plan B is to make plan A work."

I worked and saved enough money and was able to get a

car for the move. I got an SUV, which was an upgrade. I felt as if it were meant to happen like that because my prior car was my first car and a little older, but it had fulfilled its duties indeed. I got that car shortly after graduation, and it lasted until I left Valdosta.

Upon moving to Atlanta, it did not get easier. It was more expensive and way faster than Valdosta, of course. I was able to transfer my current job upon moving and added line cook to my resume. The wages were very petty and caused me to struggle with my bills and mental health. One rainy night driving home from work, I went around a curve a little too fast. I wasn't quite used to the highways of Atlanta. Once I noticed it was a curve, I slammed on the brakes and attempted to make the turn. The tires skid as I winded around the curve of the road. The car began to hydroplane, and I

took my hands off the wheel and put them on the ceiling of the SUV. I braced myself for what came next.

It felt like everything went in slow motion as the car flipped off the road and items in my vehicle flew around. Glass shattered on the passenger side as the SUV finally landed in the dirt and rocks. I hung there, still in my seat belt, fully conscious of what had taken place. Immediately, I heard voices coming from outside the vehicle as they shouted, asking if I was okay; I did not respond. I was in shock and in total disappointment of myself.

Suddenly, glass shattered as bystanders broke the window to the backseat of the driver's side. I unbuckled myself, jumped down, and climbed out the back window. I thanked them and walked off in awe. The car was destroyed, but I was unharmed. Not even a scratch.

I always thank God for my optimism and firm belief that everything is always working for me in my favor, regardless of what it seems like on the outside. We all have the capability to believe things are happening for us and not to us. All we have to do is remove all the doubt and truly believe it is working in our favor.

Doubt is related to anxiety, and breathing techniques can correct both of those lessers. Also, remember, doubt is a form of belief, too, the belief that things are not working out in your favor. When we are faced with challenges, don't forget to breathe, and breathe deep. If that doesn't work, breathe some more and breathe slowly. I remember that night getting home after totaling my car. I felt so worthless and like a repeat offender on messing up. I almost gave up. I fell to the ground in the bathroom in defeat. I had been fighting for so long and felt like the battle would be over once I moved to Atlanta, but it had just begun.

As I sat on the floor, I felt the urge to get up. Get up and show the world I am here to stay. I will overcome whatever I am faced with every time, no matter how many times. And that's what I did. I got up and smiled because now I knew what I was dealing with. I was able to get another car and kept striving. A management position opened up at the restaurant I was working at that would potentially give me more responsibilities and pay if I were selected.

Aside from being a line cook, I was also a certified trainer, meaning the majority of the new hires that came in, I was responsible for making sure they knew the correct way of doing things. The interviews went well, and the hiring managers made comments and gestures after the interviews as if I had been chosen for the new position. Once they decided on the candidate, I was shocked to find out that not only had I not been chosen, but they had given it to someone that I had trained! Discouraged, I began to look for other work while working. I was making $9.50 per hour at the time and started negotiating a raise to $10 per hour since I did not get the new position. I believe it took 2 months for them to give me that raise, and once I received it, I quit.

While working at the restaurant, I managed to get a second job at a temp agency that paid me $15 an hour to cook at various places. I liked the temp job because it gave me variety and the ability to make my own schedule. It wasn't the same faces with the same rush hour or the same dishes to prepare every day. They also appreciated my work, so they would send me to very nice gigs where I would potentially get more notice of my skills. So, I did that until I found another job. I had been in Atlanta for 6 months, and it felt like a lifetime.

I stumbled upon one more job that I would attempt before I discovered the *holy breath.*

It was a windshield repair business that was commission-only called KINGS. It was a very different job, but I felt it was good because it was different. Since I was 15, my whole work life was in the restaurant chain business. So, stepping from that into a freer workspace was exactly what I needed. Work consisted of us going to grocery stores and gas stations, walking up to random people in an attempt to see if they had cracks on their windshields. If they had any cracks, we would offer to fix them at no cost. So, I learned about the law of averages quickly. The law of averages is a principle that supposes -the more you attempt something, the higher your chances are for success. The more people you talk to, the better chances are for your yes. 100 no's do not matter when all you need is one yes.

We would receive $18 per person that we got to commit and allow us to repair the cracked windshield right there on the spot. Working here taught me not to rely on the boss to put me on the schedule for guaranteed hours. In this job, there was only the opportunity to make money, but it was up to us to make it.

If you spent 8 hours working and didn't get any clients, that was on you. (And yes, I did spend some days like that.) We would start the morning at the office and have motivation rallies. We all had to dress business casual initially and have positive meetings to start the day. We stood in a circle and chanted positive quotes together.

All of this was very different for me, and it is one quote that stuck with me, just as the serenity prayer.

It was *"Sometimes you have to jump off a cliff and grow your wings on the way down."*

And that, to me, was beautiful because that was the story of my life. Every single thing I had done up until now had been me taking a leap of faith. I had jumped off that cliff when I decided to move to Atlanta and had been hitting every branch and rock I could hit, attempting to grow my wings.

While working at KINGS, I met a now-good friend who would play a big part in my discovery. His name was literally Benjamin Franklin, and he was from my hometown (Valdosta), but we had never met before, even though we knew the same people. Ben was an interesting individual, and we shared a lot of similar ideologies. He had a company of his own, and I eventually started working with him. Ben had a moving company named Hallelujah Moving. My new friend and I often talked about God and growth. It wasn't long before meditation came up in our conversation.

Meditation had always been something I wanted to practice, but I just never knew how. Although I was doing better, it still was just not enough. I was still struggling to work at KINGS, at the temp agency, and with my friend. I stopped in my tracks, and I noticed the pattern again. I was back working 3 jobs to make ends meet. Only this time, I was in Atlanta, enrolled in college, and had a higher rent to pay.

All of these jobs were appreciated greatly, even if I did not express it properly or realize it to its true extent at that time. So, since I was in this pattern, I was once again at my breaking point. Luckily, I had help financially. My girlfriend at the time was a great help even though we were not in the best space in our relationship. In addition, my mother and sister assisted me in this fertile time.

I call the time fertile because the seeds I planted at that low point were most important. When we are at our lowest point, we have two choices: lay down in it or get up. I am also thankful that I had a friend who had been through his own hardships and came across the holy breath that changed his life just like it did mine.

Ben told me about a 30-day challenge to meditate for 30 days straight without negative conversations or thoughts. He told me if I did, then I would be able to break the cycle I was in. It was still my first year in Atlanta, but it was definitely not how I pictured it. I felt like I needed something to change. I had been trying hard to work and follow my passion, but life just kept piling it up. I was in a state of anger and resentment, and all I really wanted was peace. True peace.

So, I committed. I made a decision in my mind and held on to it, tried and true.

"I'll never be broke again" was my first mantra. I put $1 in a shoe box and said I would never spend it.

Before anything, I had to believe as if it were true. Even more than believing, I had to feel as if it were true through my breathing.

"The feeling is the prayer."

I added a few things of my own, such as cutting out social media & TV. I also added listening to affirmations (which was new) and praying more.

I feel like through all of my turmoil, God kept me safe with or without knowing about the benefits of conscious breathing. What will happen already is. Remember, some things we cannot change. However, being aware of the breath changes how you perceive things you cannot change and how you react or initiate. "Serenity"

It definitely won't hurt us to breathe more. It can only make us better. Once I gathered my thoughts, I found a chair in my apartment, sat down, closed my eyes, and took my first step toward discovering the true essence of the holy breath.

2

Meditation

Be still, and know that I am......."Psalm 46:10

My first time meditating, my brain was filled with chatter. I had no idea what I was doing but felt as if what I was doing was making a difference. My friend had explained the best way he could on how to meditate, but it is always easier said than done, of course, until you do it.

So here I was, searching for peace.

I started off with minimal minutes(5-15 minutes) initially just to get in the habit of sitting down with my eyes closed in an attempt to calm my thoughts. I would later learn that true meditation is no attempt. It is just existing and being in the presence of God. God exists within all of us. We are Human beings, and all we have to do is BE.

It is letting yourself guide you through yourself. In doing that, it allows us to discover things subconsciously that we may not have known consciously.

Prayer is when you talk to God, and meditation is when God talks to you.

It is not an easy task to start forming the habit of meditation, because we are breaking the habit of not meditating, for however many years we have lived. While it may be difficult, it is not an impossible task. With discipline and determination, we all can do anything we put our minds to. Essentially, all meditation is doing is training the mind. Early on, I started noticing changes in my mood and thoughts. The more I continued to breathe, the more confidently I spoke about myself with every word I stated after *I am.*

I am is the God presence in us.

Now, I must say this: I do not claim to be a part of any organized religion. Nor does that mean that I do not believe in it, but meaning I believe in all of it- any religion that speaks of goodwill, truth, and universal law, I believe. There is only 1 God and 1 truth, so if it falls under that 1 truth, then I believe in the oneness of it. I could never consider myself truly at peace if I have hatred, anger, or comparison in value pertaining to one's beliefs.

I believe in Christ, and I have also studied the Quran and agree with the teachings of the Honorable Elijah Muhammad.

I have studied ancient Kemet history and Orisha and Oshun truths. I have read the Torah and the Kabala and studied text from the Emerald tablets, the three initiates Kyballion to Noble Drew Ali's teachings, and Malachi York, all in search of/for higher understanding.

I choose to not identify with any particular one because a true God knows that there is only 1 God. And as long as it aligns with righteousness, it is all truth because there is only one truth. Many lies but 1 truth, and I am that. However, anyone who aligns with religion is not wrong either. We are all here to uplift the kingdom of heaven in whatever way we can complete that task. Everyone and everything has its place in this world, and whether we know it or not, we are all being exactly what we are meant to be.

"There is only one ruler. "

What we say after I am is only confirmation for what is. We create our own reality with our tongue, thoughts, and actions. But it all starts in the mind, and meditation is one way to train your mind. An untrained mind can be a dangerous mind. Untrained minds can blurt out any thought that crosses their path. This can cause them to say things they may not mean and harm others or even themselves with words.

Words are so powerful.

A person says they want to find a way to get somewhere faster and can create a whole car to do so. Another person says I am going to get fired for sure, and once they get fired, they will say, "See, I told you!"

We always have to be mindful of what we say. There is so much power in the tongue. An untrained mind can also put you in a reactive state versus a proactive state, meaning you will only react to what life gives you instead of taking control and creating your reality. We create our own reality with our thoughts.

Beloved, always remember that our minds are a gift from God.

Consider our mind to be a crystal made of gold awaiting to be discovered. It is the only *mind* that we get and the only *mind* that we truly know. It is a tough, safe to crack, but be gentle because it is yours. Remember, you always have all the power to be anything because we are everything. It just has to be realized one breath at a time.

Take some deep breaths now and smile at how far you have come through life and just today for reading this book. That is the first step to training the mind. Just by being aware, breathing, and showing gratitude. Sitting inside yourself and accepting the exact moment that we are in right now.

The breath is the ultimate teacher.

We learn through breathing. Women, while in labor, must breathe in order to expel a baby from the womb. While working out or training, we must breathe in order to regulate our heart and preserve our energy. When angry or nervous, people will tell you to take a few deep breaths to calm your nerves. The breath is the conqueror. In reality, our world consists of the breath vs. everything else. As I continued to meditate, the chatter gradually began to cease.

"In the silence, God speaks."

I learned that prayer is when we talk to God, and meditation is when God talks to us. God is the voice that speaks first. It's the notion to tell us yes or no, and it all comes down to our choices.

By now, I was meditating for 30 minutes to an hour per sitting and had really been making leaps within myself. At first, with the affirmations of I am at peace, or I am wealthy I felt as if I were faking it. The more I did it, the more I realized my affirmations were true. I am the dictator of my life. And I define who I am. I had a lot to be thankful for, and I started to realize that it was I who was not appreciating what I had at the moment. I believe that the world holds a certain order.

God rules the world, and the universe governs the earth by responding to our thoughts and actions. More importantly, responding to how we feel when thinking what we are thinking. And we sit in the center of it all, creating the reality as we go within reason of universal law. Mind you, all of this is happening as 1. Keep in mind there is only 1 God. 1 ruler. If we are all made of God:

Psalms 82: 6 I have said, Ye are gods; and all of you are children of the Most High.

Then there is NO separation between us and the creator. We are all under 1 God and 1 mind. We see through the same eyes in different variations. For example, two people sitting on a bench in a park looking in the same direction notice the same dog running out across the lawn as the owner throws the ball. Even though it is 2 separate people, they are still viewing through the one eye of God.

Even with numbers, there is technically only 1 number. Any number outside of 1 is only multiples of 1. But that, my friends, is a story for another time. Just remember there is only 1 ruler, and it is all happening in your mind. Now ye are all gods does not mean I am god over you. It only means I am God over myself. My own domain.

Genesis 2:7 ...the LORD God formed man of the dust of the ground, and breathed into his nostrils the breath of life; and man became a living –. (being)

Understand what is being conveyed in this bible verse. God breathed the breath of life into man's nostrils, and the man became a living being. The breath of God exists in us and is the reason that we are living. Therefore, God is within us, and every time we breathe, we are taking a holy breath.

Genesis 1:27-28

27 So God created man in his own image, in the image of God he created him; male and female he created them.

28 And God blessed them, and God said unto them Be fruitful, and multiply and replenish the earth, and subdue it: and have

dominion over the fish of the sea and over the fowl of the air and
over every living thing that moveth upon the earth. KJV

I can only be the ruler of my own thoughts while knowing the difference between the things I can change and the things I cannot. The key words are "I am," I never said my name ____ is God. I said, "I Am."

Remember, I am is the God presence that is both inside
and outside, as all of us.

We are only a product of our thoughts and how we truly feel about ourselves. It is partially about what you say and even more about how you feel when you say it. Do you believe it once you are done talking? Do you hold it tried and true? Do you hold hatred and spite behind the word? All of that matters. What we put out is what we will receive. It is just how God deemed things to be.

The law of cause and effect:
Everything happens for a reason; for every effect,
there is a specific cause. Hermetic Principles

Meditation is the friendly reminder that we are much more than skin and bones. We have to remember to breathe at all times. Less thinking, more breathing. More breathing means being conscious of your breathing. The more we breathe, the more alive we feel. Breathing can help you learn more about yourself than anything because the breath is flowing through every part of you-learning every part of you.

Being conscious of your breathing means you are present, and there is never a more perfect moment than now.

I can't quite remember how long it took me, during the 30-day challenge, to see a big change. It may have been around some 20-odd days that I noticed a big difference. The universe operates and expands with a flower-like essence that is always growing and changing. One day, we will look up and see that the seed we once planted is now a beautiful flower blossoming right before our eyes. A feeling came over me from within, and for the first time in a very long time, I smiled and felt truly at peace. I took a picture because I really felt good about myself.

During meditation, I would sit in a chair upright with my palms facing up in order to receive knowledge, wisdom, and understanding. As well as anything else I may have needed to obtain. Once in this position, I would close my eyes and take a deep breath. The key is to breathe. Initially, we focus on our breath, but remember the key is actually breathing.

The mind can be very tricky. A person can sit in meditation and the whole time internally remind themselves to breathe instead of actually breathing. Don't forget to breathe means the action of breathing. Even now, while you are reading this, take deep breaths as you read through.

Deep breath right here, and let it out.

Do that about 3 times before reading this next part.

Always breathe in through your nose. Sometimes out through the mouth, but most times in through the nose and out through the nose. Breathing through the nose goes directly to the brain. The nose also acts as a filter to keep out dirt and other particles that may be in the air. Mouth breathing gives us a higher cause of sickness due to the lack of filter or nose hairs.

What I noticed when my eyes were closed immediately was the darkness. The main thing I realized about the darkness was that it was something I could go further into. It was not like a black couch or tabletop that I could see the ends of due to its dark color. It was something like a doorway that I could mentally step into. Imagine walking into a dark room, attempting to get to the other side. That is how meditation feels, except the room is your mind, and the primary key is to stay present in the search for the light or self.

The light is in all of us.

Initially, thoughts would pass through frequently, making it difficult for me to focus on anything other than what I was eating later or what bill was up and coming. But that was the point. Thoughts were passing by. Who said that I had to cling to them or give them any attention at all? It's things or ideas that aren't important.

Now, surely it is significant to know what you're eating consists of or what bills are due soon, but there is a time and a place for everything. When we meditate, it is only time for meditation, which is being in the present moment. We can use other times to freely think and ponder our own ideas and goals ahead. Meditation is the time to listen, breathe, and sit with yourself. Think of your mind as the sky and the clouds as our thoughts. The sky is always present, just as our divine mind. The clouds, however, change as the day passes, just like our thoughts. Sometimes, the clouds may even block the sky out, but the sky never leaves. It weathers the storm, and sure enough, once it clears, there it is. To stay centered is to close our physical eyes, open our inner eye, and see what's always right in front of us. So, see your thoughts as clouds just passing by, and choose the ones that agree with the true you.

Another example would be to see your thoughts like clothes. Every day, we choose what we want to wear, what we like and don't like. Do the same with our thoughts. When those bad clothes or thoughts come, don't wear them. Don't try them on or out because you don't like them, and it's not a good fit for you. Someone else may love them, but this is about you and what is best for you. Always choose the higher thoughts and remember to Be gentle with yourself. It's OK, and always remember to take deep breaths and take it one breath at a time.

As I stepped into the darkness of my mind, I went through many emotions from my earlier experiences that I had not yet made peace with, from childhood trauma to realizing what I was doing wrong in my current relationships. I was able to discover feelings that I was unaware of because I was not still. One day, I was in a dark room meditating, and a light started to shine in as my eyes were still closed. The light was coming from inside! The light then covered my entire closed-eye view. Enlightenment, I felt, was the only thing that could explain it. I truly believe the light is in all of us, shining through everyone. It is always accessible as long as we search. There was nothing more beautiful than that moment.

Tears fell from my eyes as I breathed through. The tears were not of pain or sorrow, but they were tears of joy and appreciation. The magnitude of God's grace is immeasurable and beautiful with every holy breath we take. As I continued to meditate, the experiences expanded, and I found it fascinating that all I had to do was breathe.

Simplicity is key.

Our brains, for some reason, tend to make things more complicated than what they truly are. Breathing makes things so much simpler. Sure, action must take place as well, but if we just breathe, that in itself will eliminate any doubt or fears we have for our inevitable success. I could not believe that in order to change my life, all I had to do was just breathe. Mind you, this realization came to me after only consciously breathing for a 30-day period. We will not know the power of a silent mind until we master our mind.

Now, let's talk more about the breath itself.

It is a natural occurrence for our body to breathe as it is an involuntary action. If a person held their own hand over their nose in an attempt to stop their breathing, they could not because once the breath became too short, their hand would remove itself. The body's primary function is to live-and we need to breathe. How does breathing work?

The muscles in your body help airflow into your lungs. Your diaphragm muscle contracts and moves downward as you inhale, while your intercostal muscles between your ribs contract to pull your ribcage upward and outward. This creates ample space for your lungs to expand and take in air through your nose and mouth. The air then travels down your trachea and passes through your bronchial tubes until it reaches the air sacs. Oxygen is absorbed into your bloodstream, and carbon dioxide is expelled from your body as you exhale. In just one short breath, all of these things happen, stressing the importance of the breath itself.

Your cells need oxygen!

Every living thing on earth has cells, and all human cells need oxygen. Oxygen is required for cellular respiration and releasing energy from food. Our breathing muscles are controlled both automatically and voluntarily. The brainstem takes care of the automatic control during normal breathing, while the motor cortex is responsible for voluntary control.

The motor cortex is a part of the cerebral cortex. This small region of the brain can significantly impact our physical abilities, like voluntarily deciding to mediate and breathe.

Meditation is the home of executing voluntary breathing.

Since we know that all of our cells receive oxygen with or without our effort, imagine how beneficial it would be if we were more aware of the breath keeping us living.

Awareness is key.

By now, I was nearing the end of the 30 days, and I was more at peace than I had ever been. I was still working with Ben and the team temp agency as a cook, but through meditation, I was able to start a moving company of my own. Working with my friend, he saw the capability of me doing it myself. He pointed me in the right direction, and I took it from there. Granted, it took me six months to get my first job, but I started my new beginning once we broke the barrier.

Once I reached the 30-day point, I reflected on my prior months before meditating; I was working at a brand-named restaurant chain negotiating a raise. Now, here I was with a company setting my own price all from breathing. My mind was not the same as it was before. It was very silent. Where it was clear enough for me to process new ideas. Remember, *in the Silence*, God speaks.

I was more in the present moment and at peace, so grateful that God blessed me enough to not only provide for myself but assist others with employment along the way.

During those 30 days of meditation, I realized I had not been breathing properly throughout my years. I noticed that when I talked, my nose would not let as much air in as it would when I did not speak. And once I stopped talking, I would intake short breaths- not full breaths of fresh air needed to fill my lungs with oxygen for the bloodstream. During meditation, it was different (not taking in short breaths) because the point of it is to intentionally breathe (taking in full breaths). The more we breathe in meditation, the more natural and intentional breathing becomes.

As I breathed through my nose deep, I noticed I could physically feel different organs as they expanded within my body. I could direct the air/energy to a location, wherever I wanted it to go, within my body. Parts of my spine would crack as I breathed deeper. While I breathed, my muscles were fed what they needed, and at that moment, they relaxed. The tension in that area was released, and a natural action took place within my spine. As I breathed, the spinal movement (cracked/ adjusted) allowed energy to flow.

With meditation...breathing spiritually aligns, adjusting the mind to allow the essence of life to flow. As mentioned earlier about OHM. Ohm shows how God has everything lined up for us. So, as I focused my breath to certain parts of my body, I felt the vibrations, and when I focused on my body in full, my entire body vibrated. Everything on Earth, dead or alive, vibrates at a specific frequency. Each frequency vibrates and sends off wavelengths, thus keeping everything in an always-moving state.

The Awareness' is everything!

Chakras

The more I became aware of the essence of the holy breath, the more I learned. I learned that we can balance our energy by directing our breath to certain areas of our body called chakras. Chakras are different parts of our body that intake and outtake energy.

Energy is gas being released. Everything is energy, and everything is frequency, vibrating at all times. Energy also cannot be created nor destroyed, only transmuted or transformed. Quick question about energy: If energy cannot be created or destroyed, then where does it start, and where does it end?

Briefly, just to assist with understanding, there are 7 chakras. From the bottom up, the first would be our root chakra, which is near the base of the spine and represents stability and confidence. Imbalanced attributes are fear and anxiety.

Next would be the sacral chakra, which is right below our navel. Sacral chakra represents creative and sexual energy. Imbalanced attributes are repressed creativity or withheld intimacy.

Third is the solar plexus, which is above the navel and underneath the chest. The Solar Plexus represents pleasure, self-esteem, and willpower. Imbalanced attributes are having low self-esteem and/or misuse of power.

Fourth is the heart. We all know where the heart is, right in the center of our chest, working all on its own. The heart chakra represents love. Both self-love and love for others. Imbalanced attributes are depression and lack of self-discipline.

Fifth is the throat chakra, which represents the ability to speak confidently and clearly. Imbalanced attributes could be arrogance or shyness.

The third eye is the sixth chakra, and it is located in the center of our forehead. The third eye is responsible for intuition, clairvoyance, foresight, and imagination. Imbalanced attributes would be a lack of direction and lack of clarity.

Lastly, the seventh chakra would be the crown, located at the top of our heads. The crown chakra represents a state of higher consciousness and is our connection to the divine presence that always is. Imbalanced attributes are disregarding what is sacred and disconnecting from spirit.

Balancing our chakras will keep us at our best selves.

When chakras are imbalanced, we respond differently. Meditation is a way to balance our chakras. Getting to a destination is always easier if you know where you are going. We know that we have actual areas in our bodies that affect us in different ways. If we direct our breath to these areas when we are feeling down or just when we are feeling good, the results can be life-changing.

Chakra meditation starts from the bottom (root), taking deep breaths for a particular amount of time and focusing on that space until you feel it is time to move up to the next (sacral), and so on; try this and work your way up -to the crown and watch how you feel in the end. The key is to stay focused, but don't force focus. Relax. Take some slow, deep breaths, and take your time. This stuff works! If you don't believe the things you have read for yourself about meditation, I challenge you to prove me wrong by meditating for 30 days straight. *(Don't cheat!)*

One significant aspect I have learned is sometimes we don't know what we need to know. Being still and present in the moment gives us the height to see what needs to be seen rather than trying to force things. We all have to realize that we are always in control of our life. We have to clearly be able to distinguish between our good thoughts and bad thoughts.

The easiest way to do that is to rise above thought itself and realize that we are not our thoughts. The thoughts we choose and the decisions we make are who we are. Once we rise above, we have the birds-eye view to make better decisions. Sometimes, we have to step away from something and come back to it later with new ideas to solve it. So, we have to get out of our heads, choose good natural thoughts, and be present in every moment with deep breaths along the way.

A meditation story...

During my 30 days of mediation, I had a few encounters with extreme divine moments. One day, I sat for an hour while meditating in the dining room. I breathed deeply and focused my breath all the way to the bottom of my feet. As my breath passed through all the cracks and crevices of my body, I felt my spine adjust as it expanded with oxygen. I felt my entire body vibrate in a feeling that I could only describe by using the word electrifying. It was not painful but exhilarating.

As I went deeper, the light appeared and covered my entire closed-eye view. Immediately, I began to express with tears, screaming out thanks and gratification. My eyes still being closed, I jumped up and ran to the living room, and I began to do push-ups. None of this was I doing; I was in meditation. I ran back to the dining room, fell on my knees, prayed, and gave thanks while my eyes were still closed. Then I ran to the bedroom and did the same. Once I came back to my conscious self, I was in extreme gratitude for the feelings I had felt. So much power and love and mercy.

What we undergo cannot truly be explained in words, but it is real. I believe that we are spirits having a human experience, and meditation is one way to get in tune with our most high self. I would not recommend anything more in this world to a person besides God and meditation. Peace to your soul, beloved; the truth is within.

When I close my eyes, I notice the differences and similarities between meditation and sleep. The simplest comparison is when we sleep, our breathing is very deep, just like with meditation. We take full breaths when we sleep and wake up energized and refreshed.

Meditation is exactly that while being present of doing it.

Sleep itself is an interesting topic, considering every living thing must do it. Once enough hours of sleep are complete, we all feel energized and ready to start the day, just as in meditation. But there is no sleep in meditation. Meditation is the same idea as sleep, except we are alert in the moment. I began to wonder what if I made a deliberate effort, always making sure to breathe even if not in meditation. Meditation and that effort outside of meditation have kept me in a meditative state of peace for the past 8 years. And it all started with those 30 days, and I never stopped meditating.

After meditating longer, I began to feel as if I had learned and knew all that I could about breathing. All I had to do was breathe, right? What more was there? But what I continue to learn is that it only gets deeper, and in all actuality, we know nothing. There is always a lesson to learn about ourselves.

"To know self is to know God. To know God is to know self."

3

Ultimate Gratitude

U ltimate Gratitude is Key: I honestly believe even before you start to breathe correctly and meditate, just being grateful for your current place in life will perform wonders. So, in reality, step 1 is Gratitude. You have to appreciate first!

Once I completed 30 days of meditation, I decided I could not stop there. This was only the beginning, and I was determined to keep going and fall deeper into my peace and happiness.

The key to receiving is to realize you already have everything you need. It is already ours; we just have to accept it.

From birth, Inshallah, we have everything we need to function in this atmosphere. A baby is born with a brain, 10 fingers, 10 toes, a heart, lungs, kidneys, etc. We don't turn 13 and grow our 2nd heart. Everything is always there for us.

Even looking outside of ourselves, everything is already made for us. A land filled with fruits and vegetables for us to eat, cattle, crops, trees, and a location to build and live. Even what man makes himself is only a manipulation of what is already here for us. Anything built here on earth had to first be made by the material presented. All cars are made from raw materials (steel, aluminum, plastic, rubber), clothes are made from cotton and animals, and homes are made from bricks and mortar. And mortar is just sand, cement, and water.

So, what is the point? The point is gratitude!

Everything you need is already yours! Everything was placed here before us for us and will be here long after us. There is no shortage of nature. Give, and you shall receive. Give gratitude to self and to God all the time, and you will be shown what you have had all along. If you appreciate God-self, you will appreciate the God-self in others. Remember, there is only 1 ruler. It is our own minds convincing us that we are less deserving. That mindset can be easily countered by recognizing what we are already blessed with. We just have to open our arms up wide enough to receive the abundance that is ours.

Take deep breaths now and appreciate your life just as it is right now. Understand that it is your life you are living, and that is something to be grateful for. Just like meditation is a practice, so is gratitude. And the more you practice anything, the better you will get.

So here is the secret to what I would do and have been doing every day throughout the day for the past 8 years.

I thank God every chance I get.

When I am in the car alone, driving, most of that time consists of me thanking God for everything as I travel. When I am in the car with people or around people, I'm silently thanking God. And at least once or twice out loud. Gratitude is key.

Psalm 35:28 – "And my tongue shall speak of thy righteousness and of thy praise all the day long." KJV

My prayer is simple yet effective. Remember, the feeling is the prayer! What does that mean? The feeling that we express when we are asking or making statements about something is more important than what's being said. So, when we pray and give thanks, say it like you mean it, feel it, and believe it. (We will talk more about feelings, frequencies, and vibrations in the next chapter.)

Here are some **words of gratitude**- I would say and still currently say: Thank you, God, for my life, health, wealth, and prosperity. Thank you, God, for my peace of mind. Thank you, God, for my abundance; my business is booming, and my music is booming. Thank you, God, for my determination. Thank you for my discipline to do what needs to be done. Thank you so much, God, for the life you are blessing me with always.

I would continue and go into my body and give thanks.

Thank you, God, for my heart God. Thank you so much, God, for the mind you bestowed upon me; thank you, God, for my lungs. Thank you, God, for my feet, my arms. God, Thank you for my fingers, tongue, eyebrows, and eyelashes. Thank you, God, for the muscles covering my bones God. Thank you for my bones. Thank you for my nervous system. Thank you for my eyes and vision to see forward and clear God. Anything that I can think of to be thankful for, I say it, and I am thankful for it.

Remember, when you are praying, God is within you.

The only thing that keeps us alive is the holy breath, which is the spirit of God. Send the power and feel the power of God within you and give thanks. The same power that created the universe and us is the same power that is within us. Please say this to yourself out loud to understand what I am conveying: My power is God's power, and there is no separation between me and the creator."

Also, gratitude for my family and friends.

Thank you so much, God, for my mother birthing me and guiding me through life to her best ability. Thank you,

God, for all of my family: my sister, my son, my niece, my cousins, my lover. Thank you for my father and those that came before me, making my existence possible. Thank you for their abundance, God, and their love, peace, and happiness. Thank you for everyone who has great intentions in my life, God. Thank you for continuing to bless us all. You can be thankful for whatever you choose to be thankful for. Whatever you choose to say is perfect.

Feel it when you say it and believe it because it is true.

My first year was coming to completion in Atlanta, and I could see where it could go as long as I stayed at peace. Not everyone could see it the way I could at the time. A lot of people were happy I had started a company, but with us not getting any jobs, they felt it may have been best if I worked at a warehouse job of some sort until things picked up. That couldn't work because I felt all my attention was needed to focus on my business -for it to work.

Here I was, meditating daily, now having a moving business of my own, but still playing catch up financially. Granted, I was doing way better than before meditation, but this is not an overnight magic trick, I am explaining.

Remember, the universe expands like a flower blossoming that is always happening. It is a gradual and continual process. This takes time. It is trial and error of never giving up and always learning. Remember, never compare your clock to another person's clock! Everyone has their own life design they are following. Always know that you are exactly where you are supposed to be.

Take a deep breath now to appreciate the now that always is.

Every day, I would wake up passing out cards and flyers in my free time, as I was still working with my friend's company and the temp agency as well. Then, 6 months after I started the company, we got our first hit/job. Thank you So much, God! My business is booming!

When I first started my company, it was a little nerve-racking. Working with my friend, even though I did well and could handle clients, a lot of the pressure was not on me because, essentially, it was still his company. Now, with me handling my own, everything fell on me. My first couple of jobs went pretty smoothly, and we started getting in the groove of things. I had recruited a couple of guys from the Art Institute, which I was still attending, and we would knock out the jobs.

It wasn't until my 7th job & 2nd year in Atlanta that a curve ball would be thrown into play. The move went great, it was very easy. However, it didn't go too well because the client's boxed TV ended up cracked during transit. We loaded the truck, drove the truck, and unpacked the truck, so it was definitely on us. The client wanted her TV replaced, which was fair and expected. The TV cost was going to be around $1200. It was a brand new 75-inch smart TV with a curve on it. She still had the receipt with the price and purchase date on it. Now, I was a business owner at this time, but remember, this is only job # 7. The company was still building a name for itself, so our prices weren't too high, and I was still trying to get out of poverty. Regardless, I knew that in order to show I was serious, I would have to do whatever it took to keep a good name in the business. So, I had to replace the TV.

It was late that night; once we finished up, we headed to a nearby printing store because the client wanted a printed agreement stating I would replace the TV. The client initially wanted the money right then and there or by the following week. I explained that I did not have it, and at first, she insisted that I was lying because I am a business owner in moving, which is a lucrative business. Without explaining too much about my personal finances, I attempted to negotiate an agreement that gave me time to replace the TV.

A random woman who was a customer in Office Depot at the time heard the commotion and came over. She looked at me, smiled, and said today, I am going to be your guardian angel. She explained, in a way -I could not at the time to the client, that I wanted to amend the situation, but it was time that I needed. She said – "Clearly, he doesn't have it at the moment, and trying to force something would leave you without anything."

Somehow, that is all it took, and we agreed. I will say this: much of the disagreement wasn't between myself and the client. It was the 3rd party person whom the client had been on the phone with the whole time. The person who actually purchased the TV. He was unsure of my honesty because he was not there. He did not see how efficiently we had worked, only the mistake. I was prepared to give the client some of the money back we made for the job and replace the TV. The "guardian angel" said absolutely not. She explained that if I replaced the TV, then the cost of the move should be paid in full to help with that repair/replacement. She explained it could not be where she gets discounted and a new TV. It would have to be one or the other. So that is what we did.

Finally, we came to an agreement. I thanked the random woman who came to my assistance, and we left the store and headed for the bank to get cash for tonight's work. The client paid me about $500 that night plus a tip, and we agreed to have TV or money for TV by the end of the month, which was February, yes, the shortest month in the year. I paid my partner out of the money earned and told him I would handle the TV replacement.

Remember, I had not made a lot of money in life up until this time, so the agreement for me to pay $1200, in addition to my life's necessary bills, did not seem like an easy task. This was my first mishap with my company, but I knew I would figure it out. I had overcome everything else that had crossed my path, so why would it be any different now? I took a deep breath and prepared for the month ahead.

My gratitude made me realize that this time, I had an advantage. I am my own boss. I can set my own prices and do the work correctly to get the money from the client in full. So that's what I did. Back then, February of 2015 was the most money I had ever made (in my life). Appreciation is key. I appreciated the opportunity to be able to show what I could do. My business is truly booming!

It was not easy to overcome my fears, but I knew that it was either that or back to square one with no company. The most per hour I had made at the time was about $15 per hour, and here I was charging clients $50-$100s of dollars per hour. I had to breathe deeply to get more in touch with confidence. I had to believe that I was already a successful 5-star company, even though I was still just a young boy who was trying to figure out his purpose.

I met with the client at the end of the month as planned to give her the money for the TV. The client was very grateful and did not even want the full $1200. The client said $700 was fine, and she appreciated my integrity for making the situation right. The client cooked a meal for me, and we ate and talked. That situation was an eye-opener -so that I could really appreciate what God had blessed me with. Later in life, I invested in insurance and always took extra precautions to avoid mishaps.

Before starting Simply the Best Move, I would look online for ways to make a dollar. I would do surveys, write reviews, and do other odd things that paid little for the work. Now, not only was the company able to put more than a few odd dollars in my pocket, but it put me in a position to help others with employment who were trying to figure it out just like me.

That is what I call grace.

I feel like what I achieved in those 28 days, of that February motivated me in ways that will stick with me forever. I can do **anything** I put my mind to. I dedicated a whole year solely to the company. I took a break from school and did not do anything musically for the entire year of 2015. I really did appreciate the opportunity, and I feel as if, to show gratitude, I had to focus on nothing else but it. That year was my first big year, and I still appreciate those early stages that molded me to be who I am today. That year also gave the company a strong foundation. We completed hundreds of jobs, and by the end of my first year, we made around $65,000.

That is grace indeed and something that I am always grateful for. Appreciate what we have, whether it be our company, our minds, bodies, or a material thing you have worked hard for. Being grateful for something will ensure that you do everything in your power to keep it. You do not take it for granted. We appreciate it because nothing is promised to anyone. More than anything, appreciate yourself in every aspect of your life.

The following year, my current girlfriend and I, at the time, decided to split up. We were living together, and the lease was up, and we did not renew. We went our separate ways, and I went to live with a friend from Valdosta, currently living in Covington. Covington is about an hour away from Atlanta. It was 3 of us in a four-bedroom home. Living there was a big help because the landlord didn't want much from us for staying there. Due to that reason, I was able to save a lot more money to eventually get my own space. I appreciated where I was because the moving jobs were still coming in. I was now back in school and had even started interning at a studio. Everything was going pretty good until the landlord sold the house without us knowing. We were informed about 2 weeks out that we had 2 weeks to get out. The other 2 guys would go their separate ways, and I could have roomed up with one of them, but this time, I felt I had to really do it on my own.

Thank God for my Ford Fusion. I chose to sleep in my car, at the studio, and at hotels until I could earn enough money to comfortably live on my own. It was tough sleeping in my vehicle. A lot of nights, I felt like I was doing so much, but still not enough. Nobody knew I was sleeping in my car, and I never asked for help. Nothing is wrong with asking for help, but I needed to prove to myself that I could do it. It was degrading having to change clothes in the car and shower at gyms and the studio because I didn't have a place of my own.

But that is only one side of it all. Appreciation on the opposite side is seeing that I was under Grace because I had access to these things even while being in what I perceived to be my lowest point. I had a vehicle to get me around and provide shelter for me. I had a company to finance me and others as long as we continued to do great work. I was also not broke. I chose to sleep in my car because I didn't want to have to deal with having barely enough.

I wanted to be smart this time and have more than enough. I was blessed to be able to buy a gym membership to be able to work out and shower after. I was also blessed to be able to rent a storage unit and hold clothes and home items instead of having to carry them in my car. Yes, I was homeless, but it all comes down to perception. I could have easily moped and complained during that time period and never elevated from it. I would rather be grateful and see that everything is always working for my greater good.

I slept in my car for 6 months before finally finding a place I could call home. I had been working every day since

I had nothing else to do. Work, studio, and school were my routine. I also was still active in my son's life, so I would visit him frequently back in Valdosta. So, I was very grateful I had the car to keep me in a space to do what needed to be done.

One day, I got a call from a friend saying that a prominent artist needed help with their studio. Even though my passion for music is artistry, I attended the Art Institute for Audio Production. At the studio where I was interning, I also did audio engineering work from time to time, so I knew about the equipment. The main thing we learned at school is how to troubleshoot. How to get down to the basics of any problem.

I arrived at the house and saw that it was my favorite rapper! I was not star-struck as I had worked with the artist before by way of the studio I interned at. However, I was grateful to be considered for something like this. I went into the studio and started checking out the equipment to find the problem. I can't remember what the issue was, but it was an issue with their interface. Something with the connection or faulty wiring.

About an hour later, another engineer came by to look at it and told them the same thing. I was grateful I had been paying enough attention in class and the studio. They said they had to make a run and would be right back. They said I could hang out until they got back and said that there was food nearby. My friend was going to stay back and hang with me. I had been there all day and was getting hungry. I asked my friend if she wanted anything or wanted to come, and she replied no but asked if I could bring some food for her, and she would stay there until I got back. I left and headed out for food.

The restaurant was literally down the street, and it was a quick process. On my way back to the house at a 4-way stop sign, I was involved in yet again- another accident. Being unfamiliar with the area and essentially just not paying attention, I passed through a stop sign, causing another car to run into mine, totaling it out.

Remember, I was still sleeping in my car. I called my friend, and she came immediately to pick me up because she was so close to where I was. I was only a few blocks away from the house. Once the wrecker had towed the car, we went back to the house and talked for a while and realized that they were not coming back. Eventually, I called my old roommate to pick me up and drop me off at a hotel. I sat in the hotel differently than when I sat in my apartment after flipping my SUV.

I was not sad or discouraged. By now, I had acquired a sense of knowing that everything was always working in my favor. And the serenity prayer always rang out to me, showing me things that I have control over and the things that are out of my control.

The one thing we control is our reactions & action.

In life, situations will happen, and sometimes we cause them. Then, there are situations we could not have avoided or prevented, even if we tried. Nonetheless, our way of handling said things once presented is all that matters.

During this entire period, I was still meditating, still thanking God, and still taking deep breaths daily. I was determined, and I was on fire from the inside. I had just been in an environment that I used to only dream of. Even though I wrecked the car in the process, it was ok. I saw that car as a chapter that needed to be closed. It got me as far as it was supposed to get me. Granted, I possibly could have avoided the accident by paying attention, but I can only prove that theory the next time around. What's done is done. It's all about what we do after.

Now, I would have to rent a car while saving to get another car and also while saving up to get an apartment. While technically not having a real job, as some used to say or mean, I was self-employed and could only rely on what I produced. I appreciated the opportunity to once again show that I was here to stay and I could overcome all things presented.

Every moment calls for gratitude.

I lost my very close friend "Poonie" while sleeping in my car, and that was one of the hardest lessons in understanding the things that I cannot change. My brother Santonio, aka Poonie, spent the majority of his later life sick with a rare disease called Ulcerative colitis, which is a chronic intestinal disease that causes inflammation within the digestive system. He was so strong, and the irony of it all was that he actually had surgery to remove the disease and died from the healing process due to developing an infection. That was a hard truth for me to accept, especially after he had been dealing with this for 12 years since he was 18. We all felt like the surgery would give him a fresh start to live and enjoy life since the sickness kept him home most of the time.

We cannot explain how or why all things happen in life. I learned that it is always important to appreciate the people in your life. Appreciate the moments that we have with them. I appreciate my brother always and understand that he did exactly what he was meant to do while he was here. He inspired so many and is still inspiring us to this day. He was truly a pure soul. He never drank alcohol or smoked anything. He was tall and athletic. He stood about 6'5, was extremely funny, and could dance pretty well. He was not what you expected for a guy his size, honestly. I said all this to say I appreciated his life, and when his death came, it made me understand even more how important it is to breathe.

Breathing brings you to the current moment.

It is important to be grateful for a moment with a friend always. I took time off from school during this time as it became a lot to juggle because I needed to work more of the jobs that were coming in. Now, I was able to purchase another car and went on the hunt for the apartment. My friend's passing gave me even more desire to complete the mission because we would always talk about what we would do once we achieved our success. I had to continue for him. Take some deep breaths now to appreciate the life that we are living right now in this moment. How far we come is showing right now.

I hadn't had the best of luck with the apartment search until one day, I woke up and decided. I said today would be the day! I could not keep spending money on application fees just to get denied. The fees were refunded, but they took 30 days to refund, and I needed every dollar available at the moment. My credit wasn't the greatest, but it was also not the worst. I just had to find the right place for me.

I ended up finding a place in Atlanta that looked nice on the internet and decided to go check it out. When I walked in, the energy of the complex was very welcoming, and the lady who greeted me was very kind. She asked me what type of place I was looking for, and I told her, "I am looking for a place that speaks to my soul." She smiled and said she knew just the place, as she took me to one of the display rooms. 2 bedrooms for me and my son was all I needed.

When she showed me the unit, it did precisely that. Spoke to my soul. It was the exact floor, appliance color, and size that I needed. Not only that, the unit number that I would receive added up to #7. It was perfect, right, with a balcony view of the pool.

Now, remember earlier I spoke about how I noticed patterns in numbers such as 3 when I compared the years of my life. Later on in life, I learned that some numbers are more spiritually inclined than others. Three, seven, and 9 are the ones that stood out to me initially. Seven is the most spiritual number as it operates on 2 planes. The physical plane and the soul plane. (Look up numerology to learn more about planes.)

God created the heavens and the earth and rested within 7 days. Why not 5 or 6? Everything is exact for a good reason. The Three Initiates: 7 hermetic principles. A book called *The Holy Koran of the Moorish Science Temple of America: [circle] 7 gives insight...*

Even in simpler terms, 1-9, 7 is the only number with 2 syllables. Nothing happens by accident, and everything reflects. 2 syllables reflect two 2 planes. 3 is the trinity, 7 is heavenly, and 9 is divine.

For example, since I started meditating and giving thanks frequently, I also started becoming more aware of numbers that would be around during specific thoughts, conversations, or events happening at that moment. Remember, nothing happens by accident; everything has a purpose.

Numbers are what I believe to be a God language. Numbers were discovered by man, not created by man. God is the supreme mathematician, and understanding numbers around us is understanding the sacred geometry. Numbers describe where a person is in every aspect. Longitude/latitude/height/weight/age. Your time of birth, location of birth, and year all mean something. It's what makes us exactly who we are. All numbers mean something, and All timing is perfect timing. So, when I see certain numbers, I know that God is speaking through the universe. The numbers are also always there; we just have to be aware of them. There is absolutely nothing in this world that does not involve numbers.

When I looked back at old addresses, the numbers always added up to 3, 7, or 9. What I mean by added up is finding the digital root of the numbers.

Briefly for understanding because numbers are a whole book in itself, here is the definition of the digital root as mentioned in Wikipedia: The digital root (also repeated digital sum) of a natural number in a given radix is the (single digit) value obtained by an iterative process of summing digits on each iteration using the result from the previous iteration to compute a digit sum. The process continues until a single-digit number is reached.

Ex: If the numbers were 2392
2+3=5 ----> 5+9=14

Then, you have to simplify the 14. 1+4=5
Then, add the final 2.

1+4= 5+ 2 = 7

So, the whole problem would be
2+3=5+9=14 =1+4= 5+ 2 = 7

That is how to find the digital root. It's getting down to the origin of things. Doing this has given me much peace in knowing that everything is working in my favor. Remember, 3 is the trinity, 7 is heavenly, and 9 is divine. All numbers are unique and hold their own meaning and frequency. Remember, everything is one because it is all under 1 God. So, once I saw what the unit number would be if I was accepted, I knew I was accepted because the number 7 was present. A few days later, I received a call saying I was approved to move in. Not too many days after, I moved in, and upon entering the door, I thanked God for my newfound home.

Sleeping in my car molded me in ways I cannot explain in

words. But what I can explain is that I do not feel it would have gone the way I wanted -if I was not grateful for everything that I was presented with it. I learned that when things happen to us, it's not necessarily a good or bad thing but necessary. If we are able to witness whatever is happening, then we should be grateful that we can see it and know that we have the mind to change everything with our reactions and action.

Ultimate gratitude is key.

4

Vibrations

Everything is sound and frequency.
Certain sounds and frequencies will influence our actions.

What is Frequency? Frequency is the vibrations or sound waves that our body constantly permits. Our vibration level or frequency that we are on determines if we are sick or healthy, alive or dead. Everything is frequency, just as everything is energy. Frequency and energy are all one in the same. Frequency can also be sounds we hear, not only outer sounds but sounds that come from within.

The more silent our minds become, the more frequency tones we are able to hear. Every person, place, and thing gives off a frequency tone and feeling we can all interpret. The frequency also guides us, and it is right in our ears, giving us notions of what surrounds us. Becoming Intune or aware of our frequency is a way of strengthening our connection with our intuition. Feelings can also be felt through frequency.

Some people are hot or cold, depending on what frequency they are vibrating off. Hot can sometimes mean a person is angry or in a state of aggression, hence why we say someone should cool off when angry. The frequency is literally dropped to numbers that would make the energy hot. Cold can mean different things.

Sometimes, a person is depressed or lacking connection with self or others. Other times, it can mean a person is in a good space and pushing out good energy waves. It all depends. The only way to know for sure is to learn to listen to the frequency tones right inside your ear. The place we would like to be in reference to hot or cold is right in the middle. Neither hot nor cold but being just present in our highest frequency.

One thing to remember is that everyone deals with their own thoughts and problems, so most of the time, if someone's energy is off or their frequency seems hot or cold, it most likely has nothing to do with you.

The best way to assist people to reach their highest frequency is through love, patience, and understanding.

Definition of Frequency

When studying electrical concepts, it's essential to understand the concept of frequency. Frequency is a measurement of waves, which are measured in cycles per second. These cycles are defined by an object's system vibrations or airwave frequency. As mentioned earlier, this can include a signal through air or energy flow, such as electricity.

It's important to note that specific frequencies have a significant impact on our body's vibration. The International Standard ISO 2631 confirms that the sensitive range is between 6-8 Hz. If you want to experience greater personal power, clarity, peace, love, and joy while reducing physical discomfort and improving emotional stability, then higher frequencies are the way to go. Truly, the human body is capable of amazing things.

I remember the first time I felt the vibrations. It was an amazing feeling. It was a surreal feeling, the waves of vibrations on my skin. Early on in meditation, I felt the vibrations in my body. It was almost as if I had crossed over a bridge, entering a new feeling of life. I had felt vibrations before, but only for a brief period of time, like when a good singer is hitting notes, and you get the chills in your body. I never knew that we did not have to stop vibrating. Or I should say stop being aware of it. As we go throughout our day without breathing consciously, it takes away from our awareness. Not being present places us in a pool of thoughts that endlessly exist in our minds. Being aware of our vibrations can change that and bring us into the Now.

Being aware of the vibrations is a very good feeling. It lets us know that we are alive and what's for us and not for us. Not just because of what we see or think but also because we can feel it.

Remember, the feeling is the prayer.

Everything is vibrating at a particular frequency. Being aware of the frequency inside and around you can be very beneficial. The key is to relax and feel your essence. Be in you. Rest within yourself; be calm, still, and patient. As Human beings, the only thing we truly have to do is BE. When you are vibrating at a high frequency, certain things that once affected you will no longer hold that power over you.

Once I moved into the apartment, problems definitely still occurred, but my vibration understood that problems are just placed there to be solved. So, it is easier said than done, and ain't nothing to it once you do it.

Our Vibrations are similar to wave ripples in the ocean. Everything reflects, so it actually makes sense that we would vibrate. According to science, Humans are 45%-75% water. So why would we not vibrate? Every person has their own special, unique vibration that can be recognized by others. Ways to change or raise your vibration is by forming different habits. Those habits definitely include conscious breathing, meditation, visualization, exercising, giving thanks, and other positive activities. There is a lot you can do to increase your vibration, and on the opposite side, there is a lot you can or cannot do to lower your vibration.

What you do frequently becomes your frequency.

That is why it is important to stay conscious of your vibration at all times and know that you are the one creating it. High and low vibrations are both needed at all times. High vibrations without low tones can leave a person imbalanced because they may feel they are better than everyone else. Balance is key. An excellent way to balance your vibration is to spend time in nature and ground yourself, also known as earthing. Grounding or earthing is simply removing your shoes and letting them rest on the earth's surface. Of course, during this time, breathe and recharge from the home of us all.

Think of a scale or thermometer. We need the lower numbers to understand the higher numbers. But when you break it down, you realize all numbers are necessary. I say this because some people will look down on others if they are not vibrating at their frequency, but no one is better than anyone. "No one knows less than the person who knows everything" is a great quote that I learned, and I keep it in my mind at all times. At the end of the day, we are all on the same boat and only in competition with our past selves. Knowing this information can only make us better for ourselves. Of course, improving ourselves will assist those around us; Each one-teach one and vibrate at your greatest frequency.

5

Prayer

Prayer is when you talk to God.
Meditation is when God talks to you.
The feeling is in the prayer. Words can sometimes be in vain.

S aying great things without having any convicting feelings behind them are just empty words. Along with
meditation and ultimate gratitude, I noticed my life started
changing when I started to change the way I prayed. In my
earlier life, I was taught to ask God for things, almost as if I
was begging for freedom or finance only to never receive.

Once I learned that the feeling is the prayer and that
everything is in the present moment, everything changed.
I stopped asking God for anything and began saying thank
you.

We are going to talk about the subconscious mind briefly.

Google English Dictionary provided by Oxford Languages defines Subconscious as an adjective: Of or concerning the part of the mind that one is not fully aware of but which influences one's actions and feelings.

Everything in this universe has concepts of duality, as above so below. Duality explains that every left has to have a right, and to every hot, there has to be a cold. As above, so it is below showing that everything reflects. The core of Earth looks almost identical to the core of a cell or atom because everything reflects. So, our conscious mind is only a reflection of what our subconscious mind believes or interprets. It is the underlying truth of our mind. It is what we subliminally take in but influences all of our actions. I bring this up to make known that the subconscious does not know the difference between reality and what we are telling it.

That's why the way we pray is important.

We have to say things as we want them to be for them to be true and realize that it is true. My prayers changed from asking God to please watch over my family to thank you, God, for watching over my family. Even as I write this, it feels weird asking God for things that are constantly being done.

Even in the Lord's prayer, there is no asking God anything because it is ours already. We have to give thanks and command things to be made manifest.

Matthew 6: 9-13 Our Father, who art in heaven, hallowed be thy name. Thy kingdom come, thy will be done, on earth, as it is in heaven. Give us this day our daily bread and forgive us our trespasses as we forgive those who trespass against us; and lead us not into temptation, but deliver us from evil. For thine is the kingdom and the power and the glory forever and ever. Amen

Notice there is not one, please, I hope, or if in the prayer. "*Thy will be done....*" "*Give us this day...*" "*Lead us not into temptation.*" Let's break down this prayer to further understand what is being taught.

Our Father equals...The One true creator that exists in all of us. *Who art in heaven,* remember duality: if there is a sky and ground, then within us, there is the same. Remember the reference to our mind being the sky. Therefore, our mind is the heaven, which is the gift from God to make it all happen. *So, Our Father* equals, The Creator of all who art in MIND, hallowed be thy name. Hallowed equals Holy is the name. (Although spelled differently, the skull is actually more hollow than solid.)

- *Thy kingdom come* is powerful because we are now commanding the kingdom of heaven or thoughts of mind *be done on earth (in reality) as it is in heaven (in mind).*

-Give us this day our daily bread (food & finance) and lead us not into temptation. (Temptation is a mental occurrence as it deals with thought. We are tempted into doing something that does not align with our God self. We have to think about it first. Don't be led by your mind into temptation.)

-But deliver us from evil (Choosing higher thoughts will free us from evil thoughts or malicious acts that result in poor thinking).

-For thine is the kingdom and the power and the glory forever and ever (For this is the mind; kingdom, Ruler of our domain). God's gift to us that holds the power to create worlds- which is an honor, to be chosen by God to exist with God for an eternity.) Once we are connected to our silence and are present with the breath, then our wants are the same as God's.

Remember, there is no separation between us and the creator. Also, please don't confuse this thought process with self-worship because it is not. We give thanks to the power that empowers us, which is the One true creator that exists in all. It is not I or me, but the I am that gives us the power.

Remember, the feeling is the prayer.

We want to feel confident in our prayers and speak everything as it already is because it is. There is no other time that exists except NOW. There is no time coming because once that time comes, it will be NOW. Try speaking and praying everything as it already is for a week to see how it alters your reality and feelings from within.

At this moment, take some good deep breaths, Thank God for everything you can think of right now, and feel good as it is- all true.

That is the true essence of prayer.

I must say this: we cannot just thank God for a bunch of random things and expect them to come to fruition. That would go back to words that are in vain. The feeling is the prayer, so what you truly feel, you will receive. We just have to be present enough, breathe enough, and believe enough until we see it manifest.

6

Power of Belief

"They don't know the power of belief,
that's why they don't believe" – Christopher James

To believe is to have faith. I want to break down some definitions very quickly so we can understand what it means to have faith or believe in something to the core. I will show important words within the definition and define those words as well to get to the core meaning of the word.

If you want to find the true meaning of sentences or words, look up the definitions for a more in-depth understanding. *Let's start with the word faith.*

- Faith is having the highest level of **trust** in a person or thing.

- Trust is the highest **belief** in the dependability, reality, capability, and power of an individual or something.

- Belief is the **acceptance** of information confirming/verifying that something exists or is true in the mind.

- Acceptance is deciding to **receive** something given.

- Receive is a verb and is defined as the action of accepting a **presented** payment, thought, or something.

- **Presented** is defined as giving formally or ceremonially as an award to something or awarded to someone. But the root of presented is present, which means being in a particular place or the period of time now occurring.

So, to the core, the definition of faith or believing leads to just being present!

Remember, as human beings, all we have to do is be. Christ spoke about faith as well and said having faith as little as a mustard seed can move mountains. Our ultimate power lies in our belief and ability to being present while believing.

Think of your belief as a person on a paddle boat headed

down a river stream. The longer you stay on the stream, the sooner or more likely it is for you to reach your destination. So, the longer you hold on to a certain belief, the closer you get to achieving what you truly want. Belief is part of the battle, but please always remember that we have to paddle as well. Christ also said faith without works is dead.

The power of belief...

My moving company was now booming, and I had a few guys working for the company. I was now to the point where I did not have to be present in order to make money. The company was running like an engine. Ultimate gratitude is so important. I was now working at the studio I once interned as a manager. The studio was called 12 Studios and had a lot of big artists that came to record there frequently. I met so many of the big names that appear on TV shows while managing this studio. I almost couldn't believe it was happening myself.

Ironically, I was only seeing it because of my belief. I worked and helped set up big events for mainstream artists on many occasions and built relationships that would last a lifetime. I also was engineering artists on a regular basis, including some popular artists out of Atlanta.

Eventually, I decided to leave it all or change course and focus more on my sole purpose for moving to Atlanta, which was to pursue my own music career. Granted, I was grateful for the work I was doing as an engineer, studio manager, and event coordinator. My heart has always been in creating music. No matter how successful my company gets, I will always love to make music. So that is what I did and what I am pursuing.

During my pursuits and early on in life, I realized one major thing -no one was coming to save me. If I wanted to be saved, then I had to save myself. So, I dedicated every moment to becoming better in all aspects of my life, especially in music.

I have perfected my craft to a point where I am appreciated for my dedication. I also appreciate my dedication and willingness to never give up on myself and keep that promise I made many years ago upon moving to Atlanta.

I am living proof that you become what you think about and that the power of belief is real. But believing can only be strengthened by the Holy breath.

7

The 30-Day Challenge

I truly hope you enjoyed reading this as much as I did writing it. It is all truth, and I pray it makes a difference in someone's life as it did mine.

Discovering the holy breath was the greatest gift I have ever received, and I am not sure if I would have received it if it had not been for meditation. Meditation opened the door to my understanding of ultimate gratitude, the importance of vibrations, how the feeling is the prayer, and the power of belief.

Everything stemmed from meditation.
The holy breath and
The importance of breathing
are within meditation.

Through meditation, I transformed my life from a kid who spent the majority of his 15-24 years incarcerated or involved with the wrong crowd and activities -to become a respectable business owner as well as a skillful artist.

I knew no one in Atlanta when I first moved from Valdosta, and now, I cannot say the same. Meditation gave me more confidence as well as a clearer mind and vision to achieve what I knew I was created for.

I challenge the reader to a 30-day challenge of meditation.

I guarantee if you truly commit to yourself for at least 30 days, you will notice a huge difference in your life.

- Cut off all social media and TV.
- Cut off all negative/pointless conversations & gossip with yourself or others.
- Cut off anything else that is not serving your higher purpose.

Meditate every single morning for at least 10 minutes before doing anything else. Gradually increase the time to at least 30 minutes per day. If you miss a day, you must start over as day 1. It is you who will benefit from it, so please do not cheat yourself.

- Show ultimate gratitude every single day.
- Spend the day thanking God for everything you can think of for 30 days.

- Do it while you are alone if you don't feel comfortable saying it out loud around others.

Remember, the feeling is the prayer, so you want to feel good when you say it.

(My favorite place to give gratitude is in the car while driving alone and while in the shower alone.) You can always give gratitude silently in your mind, but there is power in your tongue when you speak, and your ears hear it.

- Affirmation videos help as well.
- Also, read some books to substitute for social media and TV.
- Lastly DONT FORGET TO BREATHE!

Everything on earth that is living breathes. Even the earth itself. Wikipedia defines wind as the inherent flow of air or other gases in relation to the surface of a planet.

But what is wind, really?

In my opinion, wind is the earth breathing, almost like a breath of fresh air. Notice how strong the wind blows when a storm is brewing. That is a reflection in itself that lets us know when we are going through a storm, we breathe deeper. Conscious Breathing is the best way to learn more about yourself because as you explore the world of breathing, your breath explores your body, flowing through every part of you and getting to know it better with each breath.

Remember, the mind is tricky,
and one can sit through meditation
while not meditating, just waiting for the timer to go off.

- Remember to breathe.
- Use incents or candles while meditating to help you to remember to breathe.
- Always breathe through your nose and sometimes out your mouth and sometimes out your nose.

The more you breathe this way during meditation, the more your own body will tell you and show you the correct way of breathing. If you do this for 30 days, I would love to hear your story about how it changed your life upon your completion.

Email me here: chrisjpitt07@yahoo.com

I began to become aware of my life in 2012, and I am overly grateful for the distance I have traveled.

2012 was over 10 years ago, 2009 was over 13 years ago, and today, the story is still being written. Look forward for more to come and Peace to the God within you.

About The Author

Christopher James, born in Columbus, Ohio, is a resident of Georgia, a musician, a business owner, and a father. He loves spending time with family and friends, and through meditation, he inspires to enlighten. This is his first written publication.

References

In "Don't Forget to Breathe," the internet was a vital source for reading and research. Please note that the provided links might be outdated. Thank you for your continued support.

Bonvillian, John, et al. "Simplified Signs." 2020, https://doi.org/10.11647/OBP.0205.

The Importance of Proper Breathing for Your Overall Health – Building & Empowering Communities. https://sulvfoundation.org/2021/10/14/the-importance-of-proper-breathing-for-your-overall-health/

Natural Laws of Happiness, Health & Prosperity | Happyness Coach International. http://www.happynesscoach.co.in/natural-laws-of-happiness-health-prosperity/

Jon Acuff | Give Yourself the Gift of Done | Jordan Harbinger. https://www.jordanharbinger.com/jon-acuff-give-yourself-the-gift-of-done/

How do Fish Get Oxygen, 2006, Https://farwell.glk12.org/pluginfile.php/24543/mod_resource/content/0/flvs/educator_biology_v8_gs/module08/08_03b_a.htm

Health Central, 2023. https://www.practicalpainmanagement.com/patient/treatments/alternative/oxygen-therapy-growing-research-its-use-managing-pain-flares

Kevin Courtney, ProForm, "How Meditation Can Change the Brain."2023, https://www.proform.com/blog/meditation-changes-brain/

Kathleen Rushton, Life-Giving Breathe of God 2018, https://hail.to/tui-motu-interislands-magazine/publication/ak395Yu/article/w4FS7Og

NeuRA | Studies of voluntary and involuntary control of human.…. https://neura.edu.au/project/studies-voluntary-involuntary-control-human-breathing/